T0087783

ANDRÉ PREVIN

FOUR SONGS

for Tenor and Piano

texts by Philip Larkin
and William Carlos Williams

Four Songs was commissioned by Mitzi and Jeffrey Koo,
in honor of Anthony Dean Griffey.

The world premiere was given by Mr. Griffey at Zankel Hall
23 October 2004, with Sir André Previn at the piano.

duration 9 minutes

ED 4258
First Printing: July 2005

ISBN 1-4234-0247-2

G. SCHIRMER, Inc.

DISTRIBUTED BY

HAL•LEONARD®
CORPORATION

7777 W. BLUEMOUND RD. P.O. BOX 13819 MILWAUKEE, WI 53213

I. Is It For Now

Is it for now or for always,
The world hangs on a stalk?
Is it a trick or a trysting-place,
The woods we have found to walk?

Is it a mirage or miracle,
Your lips that lift at mine:
And the suns like a juggler's
    juggling-balls,
Are they a sham or a sign?

Shine out, my sudden angel,
Break fear with breast and brow,
I take you now and for always,
For always is always now.

                —Philip Larkin

II. To Write One Song

To write one song, I said,
As sad as the sad wind
That walks around my bed,
Having one simple fall
As a candle-flame swells, and is thinned,
As a curtain stirs by the wall
—For this I must visit the dead
Headstone and wet cross,
Paths where the mourners tread,
A solitary bird,
These call up the shade of loss,
Shape word to work.

That stones would shine like gold
Above each sodden grave,
This, I had not foretold,
Nor the birds' clamour, nor
The image morning gave
Of more and ever more,
As some vast seven-piled wave,
Mane-flinging, manifold,
Streams at an endless shore.

                —Philip Larkin

III. Ad Infinitum

Still I bring flowers
Although you fling them at my feet
    Until none stays
That is not struck across with wounds:
    Flowers and flowers
That you may break them utterly
    As you have always done.

    Sure happily
I still bring flowers, flowers,
    Knowing how all
Are crumpled in your praise
    And may not live
To speak a lesser thing.

—William Carlos Williams

IV. The Revelation

I awoke happy, the house
Was strange, voices
Were across a gap
Through which a girl
Came and paused,
Reaching out to me—

Then I remembered
What I had dreamed—
A girl
One whom I knew well
Leaned on the door of my car
And stroked my hand—

I shall pass her on the street
We shall say trivial things
To each other
But I shall never cease
To search her eyes
For that quiet look—

—William Carlos Williams

for Anthony Dean Griffey

FOUR SONGS
Is It For Now

Philip Larkin

André Previn

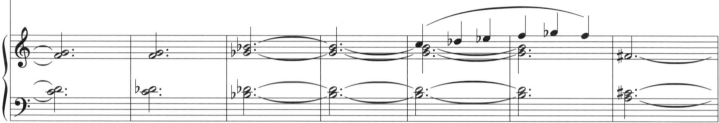

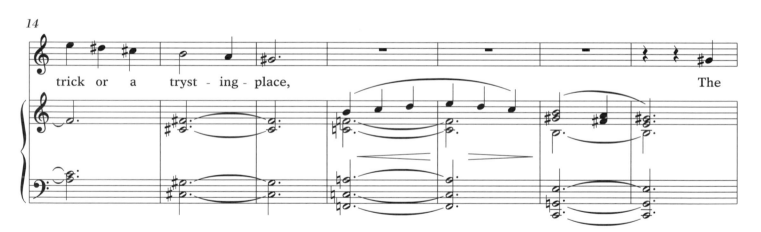

A little faster ♩ = 96

Is it a mir - age _____ or

mir-a-cle, _____ Your lips that lift ____ at mine: _____

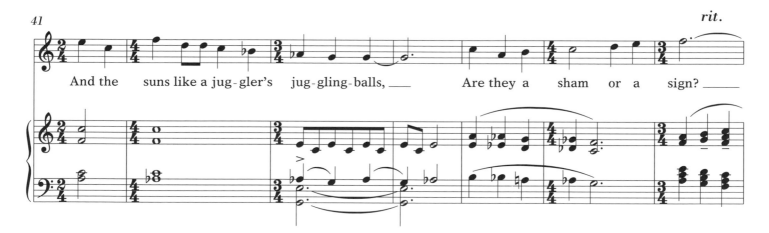

And the suns like a jug-gler's jug-gling-balls, ___ Are they a sham or a sign? _____

rit.

rit.

(f)

Shine out, __ my sud-den an - gel,

A tempo primo

53

Break fear with breast and brow,

61 *slower* *rall.*

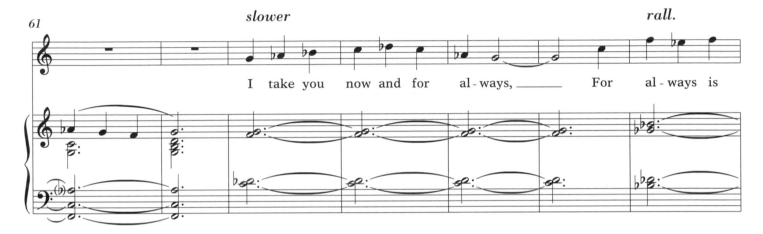

I   take you   now and for   al - ways, _____ For   al - ways is

68

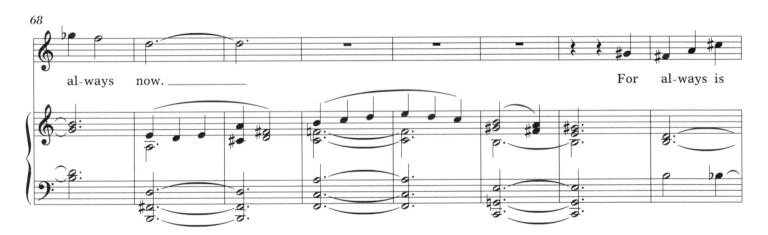

al-ways   now. _____ For   al-ways is

76 *hurry a little* *rall.*

al-ways   now. _____

To Write One Song

Philip Larkin

André Previn

Reflective

To write one song, I said, As sad as the sad wind That walks a-round my bed, Hav-ing one sim-ple fall As a can-dle-flame swells, and is thinned, As a cur-tain stirs by the wall —For this I must vi-sit the dead

Head-stone and wet cross, Paths where the mourn-ers tread,

A so-li-ta-ry bird, These call up the shade of loss,

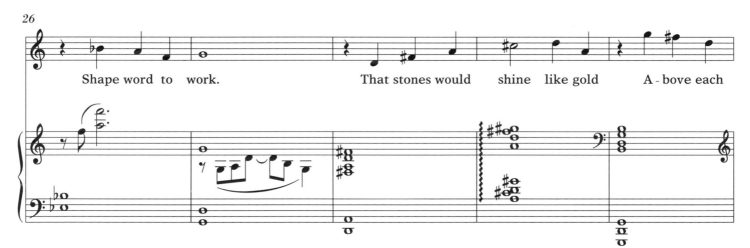

Shape word to work. That stones would shine like gold A-bove each

sod-den grave, This, I had not fore-told, Nor the birds' clam-our,

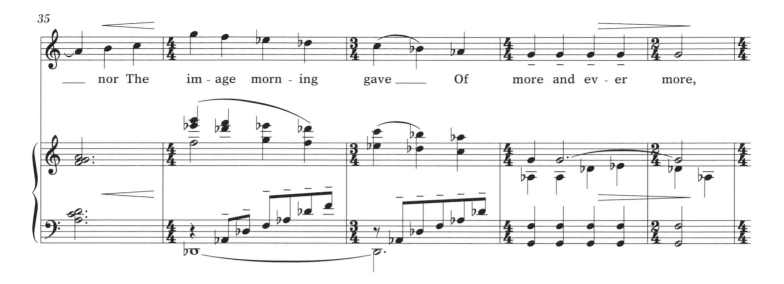

nor The im-age morn-ing gave___ Of more and ev-er more,

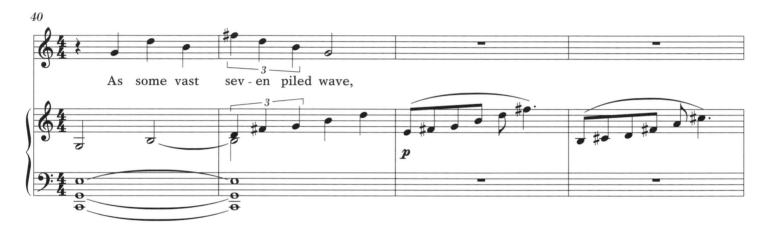

As some vast sev-en piled wave,

Mane - fling - ing, man - i - fold, Streams at an

end - less shore.___

Ad Infinitum

William Carlos Williams

André Previn

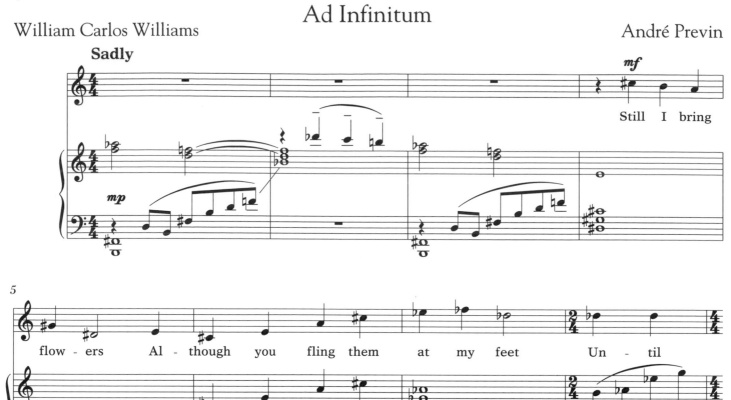

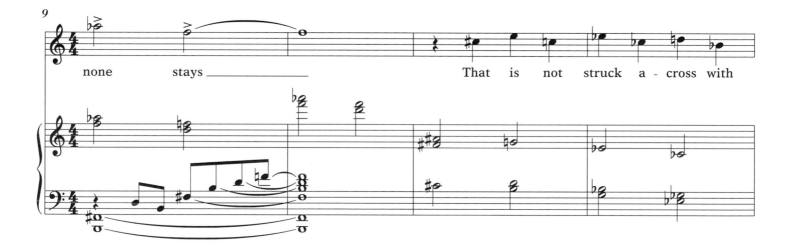

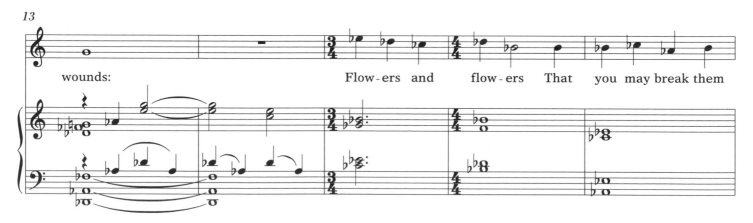

ut-ter-ly   As you have al - ways done.   Sure hap-pi-ly   I still bring

flow - ers,   flow - ers,   Know-ing how   all Are crump-led   in your praise

And may not,   and may not,   and may not   live   To   speak a

poco accel.   **Tempo I**

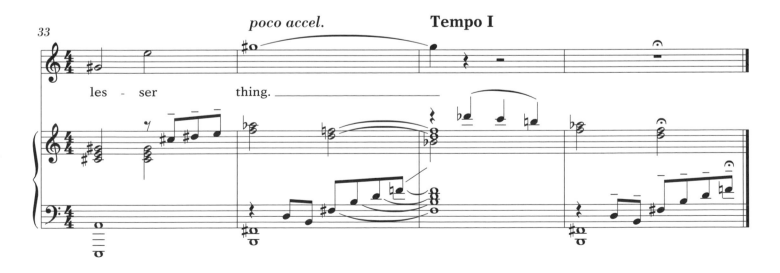

les - ser   thing. _____

The Revelation

William Carlos Williams

André Previn

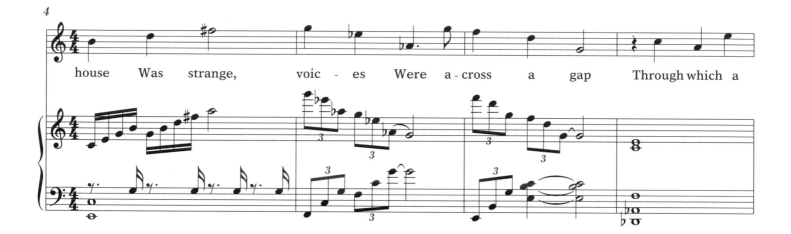

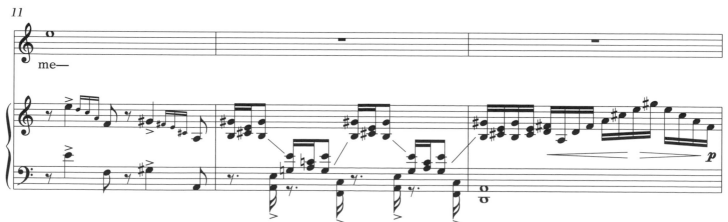

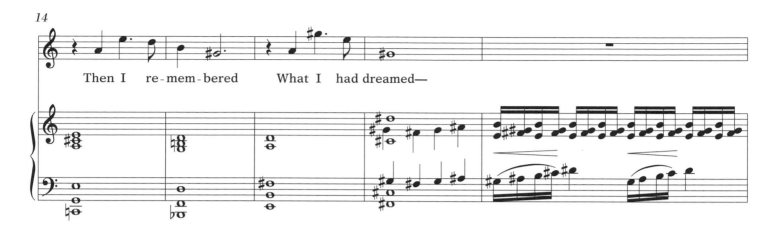

Then I re-mem-bered What I had dreamed—

A girl

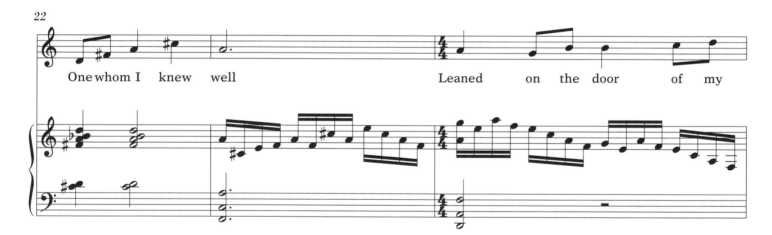

One whom I knew well Leaned on the door of my

car _____ And stroked my hand—

G. SCHIRMER, Inc.

DISTRIBUTED BY

HAL•LEONARD®